CLEVELAND
CAVALIERS

by Marty Gitlin

Published by ABDO Publishing Company, 8000 West 78th Street, Edina, Minnesota 55439. Copyright © 2012 by Abdo Consulting Group, Inc. International copyrights reserved in all countries. No part of this book may be reproduced in any form without written permission from the publisher. SportsZone™ is a trademark and logo of ABDO Publishing Company.

Printed in the United States of America,
North Mankato, Minnesota
062011
092011

 THIS BOOK CONTAINS AT LEAST 10% RECYCLED MATERIALS.

Editor: Matt Tustison
Copy Editor: Nicholas Cafarelli
Series Design and Cover Production: Christa Schneider
Interior Production: Carol Castro

Photo Credits: Tony Dejak/AP Images, cover, 34, 37, 43 (middle); Mark Duncan/AP Images, 1, 33, 43 (top), 44, 47; John Kuntz/AP Images, 4; Duane Burleson/AP Images, 6, 43 (bottom); Amy Sancetta/AP Images, 9; Eric Gay/AP Images, 11; WGI/AP Images, 12, 42 (top); AP Images, 15, 17, 19, 23, 42 (middle); Andy Hayt/Getty Images, 20; Amy Sweeney/AP Images, 25; Richard Drew/AP Images, 27, 42 (bottom); Mark Elias/AP Images, 28; Sports Illustrated/Getty Images, 31; John Raoux/AP Images, 39; Bob Luckey/AP Images, 40

Library of Congress Cataloging-in-Publication Data
Gitlin, Marty.
  Cleveland Cavaliers / by Marty Gitlin.
    p. cm. -- (Inside the NBA)
  Includes index.
  ISBN 978-1-61783-153-9
  1. Cleveland Cavaliers (Basketball team)--History--Juvenile literature. I. Title.
  GV885.52.C57G57 2012
  796.323'640977132--dc22
                        2011013804

TABLE OF CONTENTS

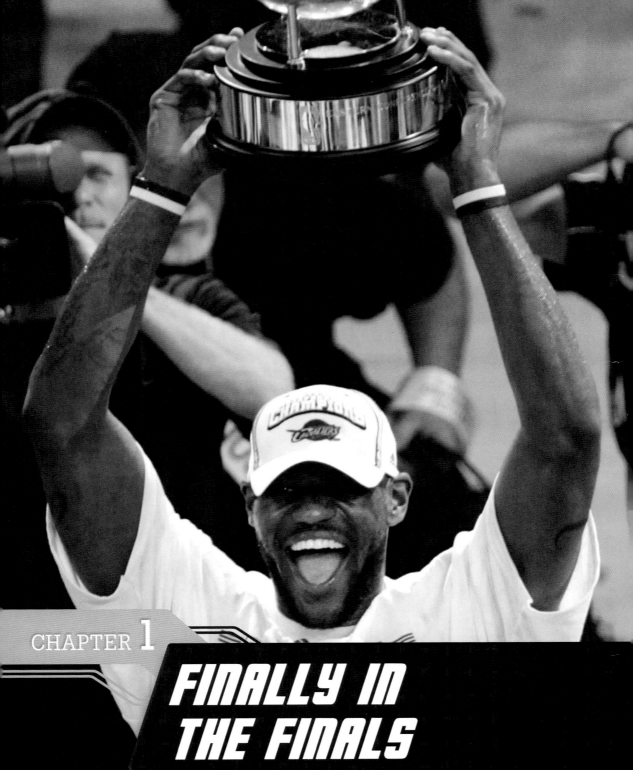

CHAPTER 1

FINALLY IN THE FINALS

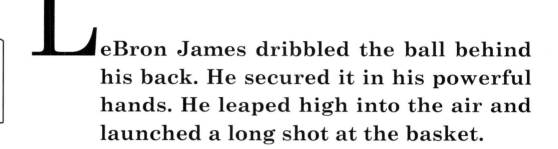

LeBron James dribbled the ball behind his back. He secured it in his powerful hands. He leaped high into the air and launched a long shot at the basket.

Swish! The ball dropped through the net.

James was red-hot when his Cleveland Cavaliers needed him the most. It was Game 5 of the 2007 Eastern Conference finals against the rugged Detroit Pistons. The series was tied. The game was tied. The excitement in Detroit had reached a fever pitch. The Central Division rivals battled into a second overtime.

The Pistons forged ahead. James answered again with an off-balance three-pointer to tie the score at 107–107. Seconds later, he weaved his muscular body past four defenders. He then drove for a layup for the

LeBron James holds up the 2007 Eastern Conference title trophy after Cleveland eliminated Detroit to earn its first NBA Finals berth.

winning basket with two seconds remaining.

The Cavaliers had never reached the National Basketball Association (NBA) Finals before. But now they were one victory away from taking that historic step. And the 22-year-old nicknamed "King James" was the hero. He scored his team's last 25 points and 48 overall in the Cavs' victory over the Pistons. The basketball world was in awe.

"King James played beyond his royal nickname . . . in one of the epic performances in NBA playoff history," wrote Greg Boeck of *USA Today*. "LeBron James refused to lose Game 5 of the Eastern Conference finals. Virtually by

LeBron James dribbles against the Pistons' Tayshaun Prince in Game 5 of the 2007 Eastern Conference finals. James's 48 points lifted the Cavs to victory.

"BIG Z"

Nobody could have predicted that center Zydrunas Ilgauskas, nicknamed "Big Z," would become the Cavaliers' franchise leader in games played. After all, he went through a series of foot surgeries from 1998 to 2002 that threatened to end his career. But he continued to fight through the injuries and went on to break the club's games-played record. Ilgauskas played 771 games with Cleveland from the 1997–98 season through 2009–10.

The lanky, 7-foot-3 Lithuanian also became one of the NBA's best centers. He earned a spot on the Eastern Conference All-Star team in 2003 and 2005. He averaged at least 11 points per game in each of his first 12 seasons in the league. He was among the finest outside shooters for players his size in the NBA.

Before the 2010–11 season, Ilgauskas left to join former Cavaliers superstar LeBron James and the Miami Heat.

himself, he dunked, shot and willed Cleveland to [victory]."

But no player can win a title by himself. James needed help in Game 6, which was played in Cleveland. And he got it from rookie guard Daniel "Boobie" Gibson. The young sharpshooter scored 31 points in the Cavs' 98–82 win over the Pistons that clinched the Eastern Conference championship. Gibson made all five of his three-point attempts.

The victory also marked a dramatic upset. Cleveland finished with a worse record than Detroit in the regular season. The Cavaliers had lost to the Pistons in the playoffs a year earlier. They were expected to lose now.

The roar of the home crowd was deafening. And when the game was over, the entire city went crazy. After all, the Cavaliers had been one of the worst teams in the NBA for most of their 37 years. Thousands of fans packed the Cleveland streets. There was much to celebrate.

"If I'm dreaming, please don't wake me up," Gibson said. "This was perfect, to win it for Cleveland."

Gibson also wanted to win the NBA Finals for Cleveland. That was the ultimate prize. No Cleveland sports team had captured a league title since 1964.

Rookie Daniel Gibson scored 31 points and made all five of his three-point tries to help Cleveland oust Detroit and reach the 2007 NBA Finals.

The city's fans were starved for a championship. And the Cavaliers were on the verge of winning one.

But standing in their way in the NBA Finals were the San Antonio Spurs. They proved to be too strong an opponent. James was limited to 22 points

Whipping the Wizards

No team played more of a role as victim to the Cavaliers during the LeBron James era than Washington. The Cavaliers beat the Wizards in the first round of the NBA playoffs in 2006, 2007, and 2008. The most dominant series was a four-game sweep in 2007. The Cavaliers went on to reach the NBA Finals that season.

a game and received little help from his teammates. The result was a four-game sweep during which the Cavaliers missed more than 60 percent of their shots.

They played the Spurs close, losing the two games in Cleveland by a combined four points. The Cavaliers simply could not overcome San Antonio's precision offense and tough defense.

Mr. Hustle

One of the most popular Cavaliers of his era was Anderson Varejao. And it was not just because fans loved watching his curly, floppy hair fly around as he ran up and down the court. The Brazil native showed as much energy on the court as any player in team history. He was not afraid to allow bigger players to crash into him for offensive fouls. He always battled hard for rebounds. He was a pest to opposing teams.

"If I don't play better, our team is not going to have a good chance to win," James said. That was the problem. Most believed that the talent surrounding James was average. Owner Dan Gilbert and general manager Danny Ferry had an important mission: to find players who could help James win a championship.

Yet Cleveland had every reason to be proud. The squad had reached a level never achieved by a Cavaliers team. The older fans remembered when the franchise was born. And they remembered when the Cavaliers were the joke of the NBA.

The Cavs' Anderson Varejao tries to knock the ball away from the Spurs' Bruce Bowen during the 2007 NBA Finals. San Antonio swept the series.

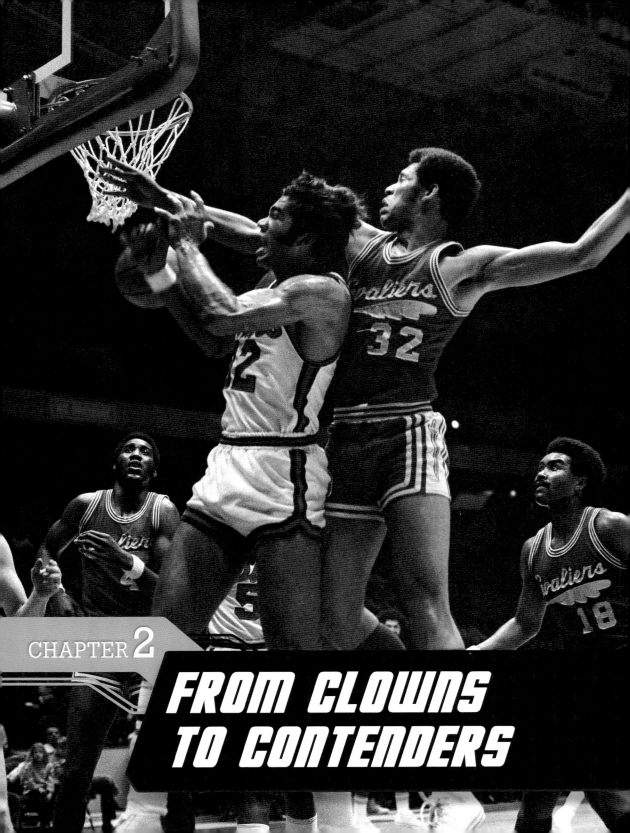

CHAPTER 2

FROM CLOWNS TO CONTENDERS

I t was 1968, and Nick Mileti was confused. The owner of the Cleveland Arena and the Cleveland Barons of the American Hockey League did not understand why the city had no NBA team.

He noted that smaller cities such as Seattle, Milwaukee, and Phoenix had franchises. Why not Cleveland?

Mileti was in luck. The NBA was looking to expand, so he placed a bid. And it was announced in February 1970 that Cleveland, Buffalo, and Portland would be added to the league for the next season. Soon after, Mileti hired University of Minnesota coach Bill Fitch to become the first head coach of the Cleveland team, which was named the Cavaliers.

Fitch had a wonderful sense of humor. As bad as his

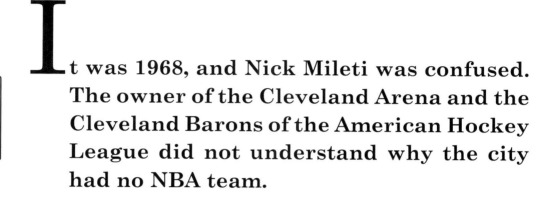

Cleveland's John Johnson, *middle right*, battles Philadelphia's Jim Washington in November 1970. The Cavs went 15–67 in their first season.

BUBBLE GUM AND BUILDING A TEAM

One of the first tasks for coach Bill Fitch was selecting players from other teams in the expansion draft. There was only one problem: He knew little about the players.

Assistant coach Jim Lessig made a suggestion. Lessig's 10-year-old son had bought some bubble gum. And in the package of gum were several cards with pictures of NBA players on the front and their statistics on the back.

"Bill told me to go back to that store and buy as much bubble gum as I could," Lessig recalled. "There were about 120 players in the NBA at that time, and I think we had about 97 of their cards. . . . We took those bubble gum cards and used them extensively to make our draft picks."

Fitch's first pick in the expansion draft was 6-foot-11 center Walt Wesley. He led the first Cavaliers team with 17.7 points and 8.7 rebounds per game.

team was, he needed it. He warned the fans that it would take time to build a winner. "Just remember," he said on the day he was hired, "my name is Fitch, not Houdini."

Indeed, Fitch was no magician. But nobody expected the Cavaliers to play as badly as they did at the beginning of their first season in 1970. They lost their first 15 games and were 1–27 by early December. Their 15–67 record to finish the season was tied for the worst in NBA history.

Though some called the Cavaliers "lovable losers," the fans were not streaming to old Cleveland Arena to watch them. The average attendance was only about 3,000 as they lost game after game. Nine of their victories were against the Trail Blazers (Portland) and the Braves (Buffalo), fellow expansion teams.

The Cavs' Lenny Wilkens, a future Hall of Famer, goes up for a shot over the Bullets' Nick Weatherspoon during a game in February 1974.

Silly Suiter

Forward Gary Suiter never made a name for himself as an NBA player. But he surely gained fame in Cleveland for his antics. Before the club's first regular-season game, at Buffalo on October 14, 1970, he was missing from the team meeting. Why? Because he was at the concession stand buying hot dogs and a soft drink. Suiter was also once knocked out cold when he ran into a door after a pregame nap.

But some players provided a spark. Young forwards Bobby "Bingo" Smith and John Johnson proved to be good scorers and gave fans hope for the future. The Cavs did improve slowly but surely as the years rolled on. They traded for veteran guard Lenny Wilkens and drafted guard Austin Carr, both of whom would average about 20 points a game.

Fitch was building a winning team based on dead-eye shooting and defense. He drafted fiery guard Jimmy Cleamons and forward Jim Brewer with their defense and passion in mind. He drafted forward Campy Russell and traded for center Jim Chones for their scoring talents. And in 1975, he traded for future Hall of Fame center Nate Thurmond, who many believed was past his prime.

Funny Fitch

The 1970 Cavaliers were 0–14 when coach Bill Fitch tried to enter the arena in San Francisco for the 15th game of the season. But the security guard would not let him in because he left his pass in the hotel room. Fitch asked the security guard if he knew what the Cavs' record was. The guard replied that he did and that it was 0–14. Fitch then asked him why anyone would say that he coached the Cavs if he did not. The security guard smiled and opened the door. And the Cavaliers lost their 15th straight game that night.

Thurmond was not done. His defense and rebounding transformed the Cavaliers from an average team to a great one in 1976. After an 8–14 start, they went 41–19 to reach the playoffs for the first time.

Fans poured into the Richfield Coliseum, which opened in 1974 in the town of Richfield, outside Cleveland. And when the Cavaliers faced the Washington Bullets in the first round of the playoffs, fans showed up hours before game time to cheer for their team.

They had plenty to cheer about in a series forever known as "The Miracle of Richfield." Nearly every game went down to the last seconds. And when guard Dick Snyder hit a bank shot to win the seventh and deciding game, the 21,564 fans in attendance went wild. They stormed the floor and tore down the baskets.

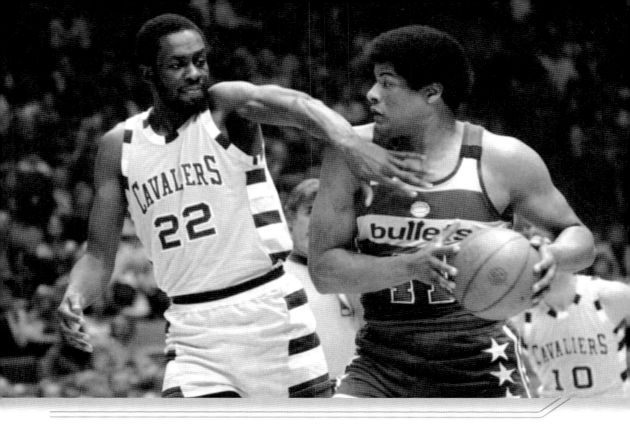

The Cavs' Jim Chones, *left*, defends the Bullets' Wes Unseld during Game 5 of "The Miracle of Richfield" playoff series in 1976. Host Cleveland won 92–91.

"I have never experienced anything like that in my life," Carr said. "It was unreal. I remember looking over my shoulder and seeing people coming at me. They were coming from everywhere. It was like a flood, like something happened. I got weak in my knees. The noise—I'll never forget the noise."

The noise continued into the Eastern Conference finals against the Boston Celtics. But Chones could not continue. The team's leading scorer broke his leg during practice before the series started. His presence was sorely missed. It forced Thurmond, 34 years old, to try to play more than his body would allow.

The Cavaliers performed with heart, winning back-to-back home games to tie the series at two games apiece. But they lost the next two as the Celtics advanced to the title round. When it was over, Thurmond cried. He knew his last chance to win a championship had come and gone.

"I wanted this one bad," he said. "Everybody did. There's no way to express how I feel. It's inside you. Right now I think I will never forget it."

The Cavaliers remained strong the next two years. But they could not recapture the magic of the "Miracle of Richfield." They were eliminated in the first round of the playoffs in both 1977 and 1978. Fitch left to coach the Celtics in 1979.

Soon disaster struck in the form of a new owner and coach who nearly ruined the Cavs.

The Cavaliers' Nate Thurmond, *middle*, puts up a shot against the Celtics' Charlie Scott, *left*, and Dave Cowens in the 1976 Eastern Conference finals. Cleveland lost in six games.

CHAPTER 3

THE DARK DAYS

The post-Bill Fitch era started well enough. Owner Nick Mileti hired the respected Stan Albeck as the new coach. Albeck wanted his team to run up and down the court and play a fast-break style of offense.

The Cavaliers boasted several young and exciting players. Among them were speedy guard Randy Smith and athletic forward Mike Mitchell. The 1979–80 team made a strong run at the playoffs with an eight-game winning streak late in the season.

But that would be the last winning streak in quite a while. In the summer of 1980, Mileti sold the Cavaliers to Ted Stepien. Stepien was the owner of a local softball team and advertising agency. He knew little about basketball. Fans were stunned when Stepien

Cleveland forward Scott Wedman battles for the ball during the 1982–83 season. The early 1980s were difficult years for the Cavaliers.

MAN BEHIND THE MICROPHONE

Radio announcer Joe Tait began broadcasting games early in the Cavaliers' first season and was still doing so 40 years later.

In the early 1980s, Tait was employed by radio station WWWE, which broadcast the Cavaliers' games. He began criticizing Cavs owner Ted Stepien on and off the air. Stepien responded by filing a lawsuit against WWWE. The court action forced the station to drop the Cavs. Tait took a job broadcasting New Jersey Nets games.

But before he left in 1981, the media began promoting "Joe Tait Night" at the Richfield Coliseum. More than 21,000 fans showed up to cheer Tait and boo Stepien.

Tait returned to Cleveland after Stepien sold the team and has been broadcasting Cavaliers games ever since. An illness did limit his work for much of the 2010–11 season, however.

hired Don Delaney as general manager. The person with that job is responsible for making trades. Delaney, the coach at tiny Lakeland Community College in Ohio, had no NBA experience.

The disaster was just beginning to unfold. Albeck, who did not get along with Stepien, quit his coaching job. Stepien replaced him with the unpopular Bill Musselman. Musselman worked the players too hard but was often late showing up to practice himself. The Cavaliers collapsed. They suffered through losing streaks of seven, eight, and nine games during the 1980–81 season.

Stepien was better at promoting the team than running it. He traded his top college draft picks for average veteran players. His trades were so terrible that the NBA

The Cavaliers' James Silas, *left*, attempts to drive against the Kings' Leon Douglas in January 1982. Cleveland went an NBA-worst 15–67 during the 1981–82 season.

banned him from making deals unless they were approved by the league.

The Cavaliers hit rock bottom in 1982 when they matched their first season with a 15–67 record. They played worse as the season progressed and finished it with a 19-game losing streak.

Stepien brought in several coaches to stop the bleeding. He even put Delaney into that role, but with no success.

By 1983, Stepien had lost an estimated $15 million as owner. The seats at Richfield Coliseum were empty. He threatened to move the team to

Bad Idea

Ted Stepien was a better promoter than team owner. But in the summer of 1980 he organized a stunt that turned out to be a disaster. Stepien arranged to have softballs thrown off the Terminal Tower, the tallest building in Cleveland at 708 feet (216 m). Members of his Cleveland Competitors softball team would catch them. The softballs would be falling at 144 miles per hour (231.7 kilometers per hour). A crowd of 5,000 showed up, but the softballs did not travel straight down. The first hit the hood of a car. The next hit a spectator in the shoulder. The third broke a woman's wrist.

Toronto. He even went to that Canadian city to announce on a radio sports talk show his plans to turn the Cleveland Cavaliers into the Toronto Towers.

Stepien somehow thought he could keep the announcement secret from Cleveland fans. But Cleveland radio sports talk show host Pete Franklin found out about it and called the Toronto radio show while Stepien was on the air. Franklin disguised his voice to pretend he was a small boy.

"Am I talking to the dumbest man in professional sports?" Franklin asked Stepien.

"I don't know what would make you say that," Stepien replied.

Franklin then screamed at Stepien in his real voice, calling him a "two-faced liar."

Stepien did not move the team to Toronto. Brothers George and Gordon Gund, who owned the Richfield Coliseum, bought the club from Stepien. But first the NBA promised them the return of the draft picks Stepien had traded away.

The Gunds hired respected George Karl as the new coach. The Cavaliers lost 19 of their first 21 games to start the 1984–85 season. But suddenly they caught fire behind a flamboyant guard who had changed

Cleveland's World B. Free rises for a shot as Boston's Kevin McHale defends him in April 1985. Free helped the Cavs reach the playoffs that year.

his name from Lloyd Free to World B. Free.

Free led the team into the playoffs, and his talent and exciting style also brought fans back to the arena. Some still believe he saved the franchise. The Cavaliers lost to powerful Boston in the first round of the playoffs, but Free had led the team back to respectability.

"The important thing was we were then poised to become a pretty good basketball team," said general manager Harry Weltman. "We had won 36

The Wrong Choice

The 1985 college draft was approaching. And Cavaliers general manager Harry Weltman had narrowed his choices to power forwards Keith Lee and Karl Malone. Weltman decided to make a trade with the Chicago Bulls to ensure the Cavaliers could select Lee. That was a terrible mistake. Lee had a short NBA career. Malone was drafted by the Utah Jazz and became one of the finest players in league history.

games, and had we gotten past Boston I think we probably would have gone all the way to the NBA Finals. I really believe that. It was some turnaround. I was really proud of those guys."

That pride would quickly grow for the fans, but Weltman and Karl were not around to enjoy it. Both were fired as the Gunds hired Lenny Wilkens as coach and Wayne Embry as general manager. Wilkens had already won an NBA championship as coach of the Seattle SuperSonics.

By late 1986, Embry had built a team that would bloom into a title contender. He drafted young stars such as center Brad Daugherty and guard Ron Harper. He also pulled off a trade with the Dallas Mavericks to land rookie guard Mark Price. The Cavaliers were about to embark on their finest era to date.

NBA commissioner David Stern, *left*, stands with Brad Daugherty in June 1986 after the Cavs drafted Daugherty first overall. Daugherty would excel for Cleveland for many years.

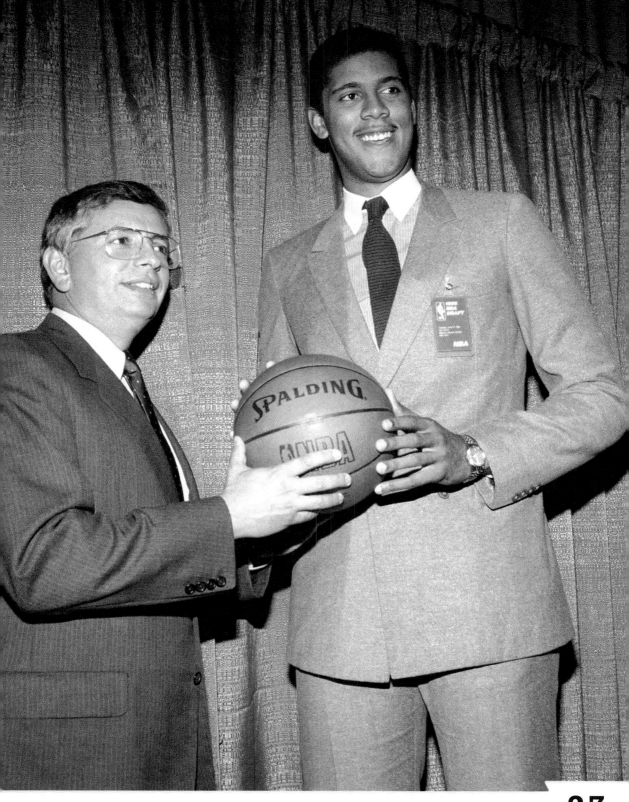

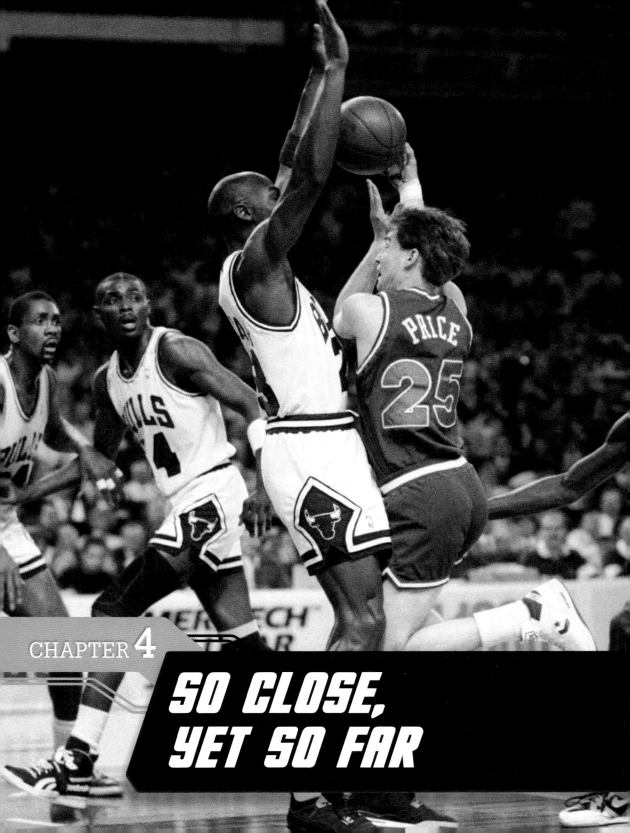

CHAPTER 4

SO CLOSE, YET SO FAR

Greatness appeared right around the corner for the Cavaliers in the late 1980s. They boasted young talent who had never played together, so it took a couple of years for the team to excel.

But the Cavs did just that in the spring of 1988. They won 11 of their last 13 regular-season games to reach the playoffs.

Though they lost in the first round to Chicago, there was reason for optimism.

The Cavaliers looked unbeatable the following season. By that time, forward Larry Nance had been added to the roster. Nance brought veteran leadership. By early March, the Cavaliers owned the NBA's best record at 43–12. But they did not perform as well down the stretch. They finished the year 57–25. Yet most believed they would blast the Bulls in the first round of the playoffs. After all, they had beaten Chicago all six times they had met that season.

The Bulls' Michael Jordan had other ideas. He was a one-man gang as Chicago forced a

The Bulls' Michael Jordan blocks an attempted shot by the Cavaliers' Mark Price in a 1989 playoff game. Chicago often stood in Cleveland's way during that era.

THE BEST BEFORE LEBRON?

Who is the best player in Cavaliers history aside from LeBron James? That question has been debated. But a frequent choice is Mark Price.

General manager Wayne Embry wanted the Georgia Tech sharpshooter badly in 1986. So after Dallas drafted him, he sent $50,000 and a second-round pick to the Mavericks for Price. Embry would never regret that deal.

Price averaged between 15 and 20 points a game every season from 1988 to 1995. He was also one of the finest foul shooters in NBA history and a great passer.

Until James arrived in 2003, Price was the only player in Cavaliers history to be named to the All-NBA first team. He earned that honor in 1993 after averaging 18.2 points and eight assists per game. He also led the league by hitting nearly 95 percent of his foul shots.

fifth and deciding game at the Richfield Coliseum.

It was not Brad Daugherty, Mark Price, or Nance who kept the Cavaliers alive. It was guard Craig Ehlo, who hit three three-pointers in the fourth quarter. The last one gave his team a 98–97 lead with 52 seconds left. Jordan and Ehlo then traded baskets. The Cavaliers led 100–99 with just three seconds remaining.

The Bulls had one chance to win the game and the series. Everyone knew who would take the last shot: Jordan.

Jordan looked at Cleveland coach Lenny Wilkens and smiled. The Bulls' star grabbed a pass from teammate Brad Sellers as Ehlo

The Bulls' Michael Jordan gets ready to release "The Shot" over the Cavs' Craig Ehlo as Larry Nance, *right*, looks on during the 1989 playoffs.

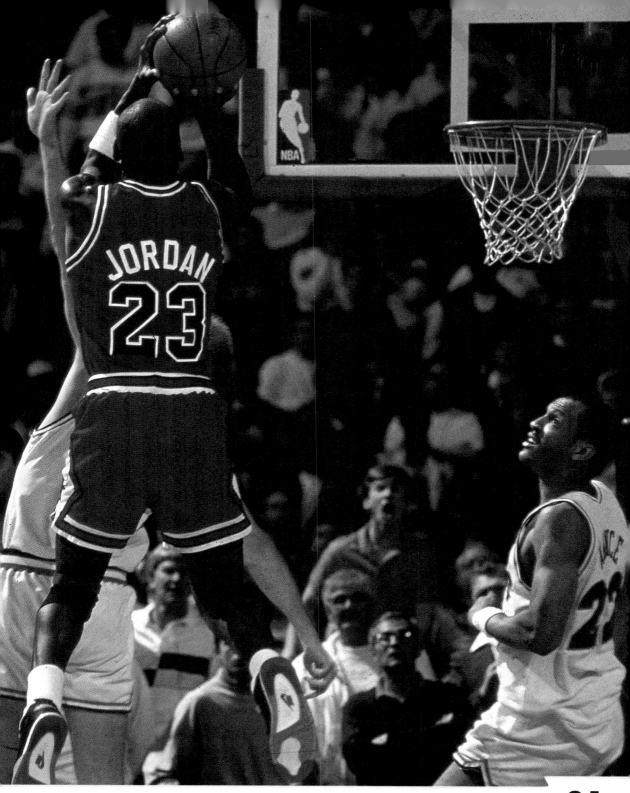

"We jumped at [Jordan] as he shot and made him change his shot in mid-air, and still. . . . I can't fathom how in the world our season has ended," Daugherty said.

Jordan became more amazing with time. And he grew into a bigger pest for the Cavaliers.

Many believe trading Ron Harper the next season prevented the Cavaliers from winning an NBA title. General manager Wayne Embry added two top college draft picks in the trade to the Los Angeles Clippers for forward Danny Ferry. Ferry proved to be only an average player.

The Cavaliers again had won 57 games as the 1992 playoffs opened. They then defeated the New Jersey Nets and the Boston Celtics to reach the Eastern Conference finals.

The Bulls awaited them. And Jordan clobbered them. He

stayed with him step for step. Jordan launched a 20-foot shot over Ehlo's outstretched arm. The arena was silent as the ball floated through the air. And it remained silent as it went through the net.

The Cavaliers had lost the game and the series. They were doomed by what would be forever known simply as "The Shot." And when it was over, they were stunned.

Cleveland's Craig Ehlo drives against Chicago's Michael Jordan during the 1992 Eastern Conference finals. The Bulls beat the Cavs in six games.

averaged 32 points as Chicago beat Cleveland in six games. The next year, he scored 31 points per game in the second round of the playoffs to lead a Bulls sweep of the Cavaliers.

Soon Price, Daugherty, and Nance were gone. And the greatest era of Cavaliers basketball slipped away without a championship.

The Cavaliers enjoyed some strong seasons as the 1990s progressed. But they simply were not talented enough to contend for a title. Early in the next decade, one player returned hope that an NBA crown could be won. That player was LeBron James.

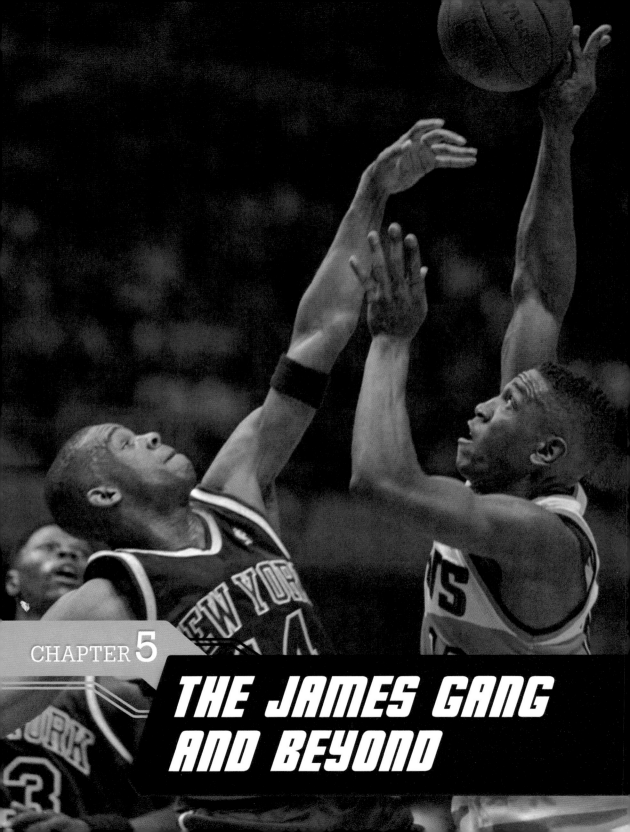

CHAPTER 5

THE JAMES GANG AND BEYOND

Nobody was surprised that the Cavaliers played great defense from 1993 to 1999. That is because Mike Fratello had replaced Lenny Wilkens as coach.

Fratello slowed down the pace of the game. His teams walked the ball up and down the floor. In many games, both teams scored fewer than 90 or even 80 points. Defensive-minded players such as Bobby Phills, Chris Mills, and Tyrone Hill often shut down opponents. Point guard Terrell Brandon was one of the few consistent scorers.

One exception was forward Shawn Kemp. The Cavaliers traded Brandon and Hill to acquire the former Seattle SuperSonics superstar. Cleveland signed him to a seven-year contract for more than $100 million. The deal

The Knicks' Hubert Davis blocks the Cavaliers' Bobby Phills, *right*, during the 1995 playoffs. Cleveland lost that series. It was one of four first-round defeats in a five-season stretch under coach Mike Fratello.

Tragic Accident

Bobby Phills was an average player for the Cavaliers from 1991 to 1997. But he was respected as a person who loved his wife and two daughters. Phills, however, also loved fast cars, and that cost him his life. On January 12, 2000, Phills was speeding down the road when he lost control of his sports car. He skidded into another car and was killed.

was a disaster. Kemp was overweight and already on the decline. He had just one decent season with the Cavs.

Fratello coached Cleveland to five straight winning seasons and four playoff berths. But the Cavaliers simply were not strong enough to advance. They had a combined record of 2–12 in losing in the first round of every playoff series.

By the end of the Fratello era, the Cavaliers and their fans began hearing about an amazing young talent in nearby Akron, Ohio. His name was LeBron James. James quickly earned a reputation as one of the best high school players in US history.

The Cavs had a terrible 2002–03 season. They finished with a 17–65 record that was the worst in the league. That ended up working in their favor. The annual NBA Draft gives the top choices to the teams with the worst records the previous season. James had already announced he would skip college to enter the NBA. And when the Cavaliers secured the first pick in the draft by winning the annual draft lottery, they chose the local star.

As a rookie in the 2003–04 season, James showed immediately that he could do everything well on the court. Only 18 years old at the beginning of the season, he was already one of the NBA's best passers. He was both quick and powerful. He

LeBron James holds up his new jersey the day after the Cavaliers selected the Ohio high school star with the top pick in the 2003 NBA Draft.

could drive to the basket and dunk on defenders, even tall ones. He averaged 20.9 points per game as a rookie with the Cavs, a tremendous feat for a teenager.

"He's unbelievable, incredible really," said Orlando Magic star Tracy McGrady. "He has that swagger. Nothing rattles him at all. He's got extremely high confidence, and he's a real competitor. At the age of 19, that's scary."

The Cavaliers spent the next seven years trying to surround James with players who could help him win a championship. Team owner Dan Gilbert and general manager Danny Ferry hired a new coach in Mike Brown, who improved the team's defense. In 2005, the Cavs signed guard Larry Hughes, who was coming off his finest season with the Washington Wizards. Hughes helped the Cavaliers reach the NBA Finals in 2007, but he never played as well as he had with the Wizards.

It seemed that the addition of point guard Mo Williams before the 2008–09 season would put Cleveland over the top. The Cavaliers finished with an NBA-best 66–16 record. They won their first two play-off rounds against Detroit and Atlanta without losing a game. In fact, they won all eight games by at least 10 points.

The Cavs then built a 39–24 lead in the first game of the Eastern Conference finals against the visiting Orlando Magic. Cleveland appeared un-stoppable. But Orlando climbed back into the game and won

it on a basket with 14 seconds left. James answered with a game-winning shot in the last second of Game 2. But the Cavaliers could not beat the Magic in Orlando and lost the series in six games.

The Cavs had thought they were on their way to a championship. And when it was over, they were crushed.

"It's very disappointing," said Zydrunas Ilgauskas, a center who had been with the team since 1997. "It just goes to show that you can't take anything for granted. You can have the best record in the regular season, and it means nothing. You've still got to go out and play in the playoffs. We're very disappointed, and it's going to be a long summer."

It would not be their last long summer. The Cavaliers finished the following season again with the best record in

The Cavs' LeBron James drives against the Magic's Mickael Pietrus during the 2009 Eastern Conference finals. Cleveland had the NBA's best regular-season record but fell to Orlando in six games.

the NBA. But this time they lost in the second round to the Boston Celtics. For the first time in the postseason, James played poorly.

The summer of 2010 was tense not only because of that defeat. The team and its fans were nervous because James was a free agent. He could sign a contract to play for any team. The Cavaliers hoped he would return. James announced his decision on national TV.

LeBron James waits in July 2010 to make an announcement on national television that he is leaving the Cavaliers to sign with the Heat.

Offense or Defense?

During the LeBron James era, coach Mike Brown and general manager Danny Ferry were not on the same page. Brown wanted a team that played tight defense. But Ferry brought in standout scorers in Mo Williams and Antawn Jamison. Neither was known for being a strong defensive player. In the 2010 playoffs, Cleveland played poor defense in losing to Boston.

"This fall, I'm going to take my talents to South Beach and join the Miami Heat," he told the nation.

Gilbert was angry and frustrated. The owner wrote a letter accusing James of betraying the city and the team's fans. Gilbert claimed that the Cavaliers would win an NBA title before James did. He later stated that James quit on the team in the playoff series against Boston.

Most fans did not believe the Cavaliers would win a title before James did. The team struggled in its first season without James. Cleveland suffered a 26-game losing streak, the longest in NBA history.

Nobody could predict what would happen to the Cavaliers in the future. They appeared to once again be a long way from contending for a championship. But Cavaliers fans hope they will soon find another star to take them to the top.

SHAKING THINGS UP

Cavaliers owner Dan Gilbert tried everything to convince superstar LeBron James to stay in Cleveland after the 2009–10 season. Nothing worked.

Gilbert fired Mike Brown as coach and hired Byron Scott as his replacement. Gilbert believed James wanted to work with a coach who had played in the NBA.

Before hiring Scott, Gilbert offered the job to Michigan State University coach Tom Izzo. But Izzo turned it down. Some believe he would have accepted the coaching spot if he knew that James would remain with the Cavaliers.

Brown was not the only loss. General manager Danny Ferry also resigned. Among the players who left along with James was Shaquille O'Neal. The Cavs signed O'Neal before the 2009–10 season, but he spent much of the campaign injured. He joined Boston after the season.

TIMELINE

1970 It is announced on February 6 that Cleveland is receiving an NBA franchise starting with the 1970–71 season. Bill Fitch is named the team's first coach on March 18. On November 12, the Cavaliers record their first victory after 15 straight losses with a 105–103 win over the host Portland Trail Blazers.

1974 The Cavaliers play their first game at the Richfield Coliseum on October 29. They lose 107–92 to the Boston Celtics.

1976 On April 29, the Cavaliers clinch a victory in their first playoff series. They defeat the visiting Washington Bullets 87–85 in the seventh and deciding game.

1979 Fitch leaves to coach Boston after nine seasons in Cleveland.

1980 Ted Stepien buys the Cavaliers from Nick Mileti in the summer. His ownership proves to be a disaster.

1983 Gund brothers Gordon and George purchase the Cavaliers from Stepien and turn the team around.

1985 Flashy guard World B. Free leads the host Cavaliers to a 105–98 first-round playoff win over the mighty Celtics on April 23. Boston would win the series three games to one, but Cleveland's victory highlighted the team's comeback from the Stepien era.

1986 The Cavs select center Brad Daugherty and guard Ron Harper and trade for Mark Price in the June 17 NBA Draft. Those players would lead the team during its finest era until LeBron James arrived. Former Cavaliers star player Lenny Wilkens becomes coach of the team in June. He would become the first winning coach in club history.

1989	Chicago superstar Michael Jordan hits "The Shot" on May 7 to give the visiting Bulls a series-clinching 101–100 victory over the Cavaliers. Cleveland is upset three games to two in the first round of the playoffs.
1992	Cleveland wins two playoff rounds for the first time in team history, defeating the New Jersey Nets and Boston. But the Cavaliers fall four games to two to the Bulls in the Eastern Conference finals.
1997	On November 10, former Seattle SuperSonics star forward Shawn Kemp signs a seven-year contract with the Cavaliers worth more than $100 million. Kemp proves to be a bitter disappointment with Cleveland.

2003	The Cavaliers select Akron, Ohio, native LeBron James straight out of high school with the first pick in the NBA Draft on June 26. James becomes easily the team's best player ever.
2007	James scores the Cavs' last 25 points in their double-overtime victory over the host Detroit Pistons on May 31 in Game 5 of the Eastern Conference finals. James finishes the game with 48 points. The Cavaliers clinch their first NBA Finals berth on June 2 with a Game 6 victory over visiting Detroit. Guard Daniel Gibson scores 31 points for the Cavaliers. However, the San Antonio Spurs sweep Cleveland in four games in the Finals.
2010	Owner Dan Gilbert announces on July 1 that Byron Scott is the new Cavaliers coach. James, a free agent, announces on national television on July 8 that he is leaving the Cavaliers to play for the Miami Heat. His decision leaves millions of Cavaliers fans frustrated and angry.

QUICK STATS

FRANCHISE HISTORY

1970–

NBA FINALS

2007

CONFERENCE FINALS

1976, 1992, 2007, 2009

DIVISION CHAMPIONSHIPS

1976, 2009, 2010

PLAYOFF APPEARANCES

1976, 1977, 1978, 1985, 1988, 1989, 1990, 1992, 1993, 1994, 1995, 1996, 1998, 2006, 2007, 2008, 2009, 2010

KEY PLAYERS
(position[s]; years with team)

Terrell Brandon (G; 1991–97)
Austin Carr (G; 1971–80)
Jim Chones (C; 1974–79)
Brad Daugherty (C; 1986–94)
World B. Free (G; 1982–86)
Ron Harper (G; 1986–89)
Zydrunas Ilgauskas (C; 1997–2010)
LeBron James (G/F; 2003–10)
Mike Mitchell (F; 1978–81)
Larry Nance (F; 1988–94)
Mark Price (G; 1986–95)
Bobby "Bingo" Smith (F; 1970–79)
John "Hot Rod" Williams (F; 1986–95)
Mo Williams (G; 2008–2011)

KEY COACHES

Mike Brown (2005–10):
    272–138; 42–29 (postseason)
Lenny Wilkens (1986–93):
    316–259; 18–23 (postseason)

HOME ARENAS

Cleveland Arena (1970–74)
Richfield Coliseum (1974–93)
Quicken Loans Arena (1994–)
    Known as Gund Arena
    (1994–2005)

* All statistics through 2010–11 season

QUOTES AND ANECDOTES

Legendary Cavaliers announcer Joe Tait has said the most thrilling game he ever broadcast was not even a playoff game. It was Cleveland's regular-season home game on January 29, 1980, against the powerful Los Angeles Lakers. It took four overtimes for the Cavaliers to stun the Lakers 154–153. The game tied for the longest in franchise history. Forward Mike Mitchell clinched the victory with two seconds left in the fourth overtime by making two foul shots.

"Some of the things he does are like in a video game. You think, 'You can't do that in real life.' I've seen a lot of great performances and guys score over 50, but not in a pressure situation like tonight in a game that means so much to an organization." —Cavaliers center Scot Pollard, after teammate LeBron James scored Cleveland's final 25 points, and 48 in all, in the team's 109–107, double-overtime victory over the host Detroit Pistons in Game 5 of the 2007 Eastern Conference finals

Through the 2009–10 season, a Cavaliers player had scored 47 or more points in a game 15 times. It was LeBron James on 14 of those occasions. James set a franchise record by scoring 56 points against the host Toronto Raptors on March 20, 2005. Center Rick Roberson owned the team record for most rebounds in a game with 25 against the host Houston Rockets on March 4, 1972. Guard Geoff Huston set the mark for most assists in a game with 27 against the visiting Golden State Warriors on January 27, 1982.

LeBron James became the Cavaliers' first NBA scoring champion in 2008 by finishing the season averaging 30.0 points a game. He was also the first Cavs player to win league MVP honors. He won that award in both 2009 and 2010.

GLOSSARY

assist

A pass that leads directly to a made basket.

attendance

The number of fans at a particular game or who come to watch a team play during a particular season.

berth

A place, spot, or position, such as in the NBA playoffs.

contract

A binding agreement about, for example, years of commitment by a basketball player in exchange for a given salary.

draft

A system used by professional sports leagues to select new players in order to spread incoming talent among all teams. The NBA Draft is held each June.

expansion

In sports, the addition of a franchise or franchises to a league.

franchise

An entire sports organization, including the players, coaches, and staff.

free agent

A player whose contract has expired and who is able to sign with a team of his choice.

general manager

The executive who is in charge of the team's overall operation. He or she hires and fires managers and coaches, drafts players, and signs free agents.

overtime

A period in a basketball game that is played to determine a winner when the four quarters end in a tie.

rebound

To get control of the basketball after a missed shot.

trade

A move in which a player or players are sent from one team to another.

FOR MORE INFORMATION

Further Reading

Ballard, Chris. *The Art of a Beautiful Game: The Thinking Fan's Tour of the NBA*. New York: Simon & Schuster, 2009.

Knight, Jonathan. *Classic Cavs: The 50 Greatest Games in Cleveland Cavaliers History*. Kent, OH: Kent State University Press, 2009.

Pluto, Terry, and Brian Windhorst. *LeBron James: The Making of an MVP*. Cleveland: Gray & Co., 2009.

Web Links

To learn more about the Cleveland Cavaliers, visit ABDO Publishing Company online at **www.abdopublishing.com**. Web sites about the Cavaliers are featured on our Book Links page. These links are routinely monitored and updated to provide the most current information available.

Places to Visit

Greater Cleveland Sports Hall of Fame

Cleveland Public Auditorium
500 Lakeside Avenue
Cleveland, OH 44114
216-682-0141
http://clevelandsportshall.com
This hall of fame pays tribute to the greatest athletes in the Cleveland area's history. Former Cavaliers Austin Carr and Jim Chones are among those honored.

Naismith Memorial Basketball Hall of Fame

1000 West Columbus Avenue
Springfield, MA 01105
413-781-6500
www.hoophall.com
This hall of fame and museum highlights the greatest players and moments in the history of basketball. Nate Thurmond and Lenny Wilkens are among the former Cavaliers players enshrined here.

Quicken Loans Arena

1 Center Court
Cleveland, OH 44115
1-800-820-2287
www.theqarena.com
This has been the Cavaliers' home arena since 1994.

INDEX

About the Author

Marty Gitlin is a freelance writer based in Cleveland, Ohio. He has written more than 35 educational books. Gitlin has won more than 45 awards in his 25 years as a writer, including first place for general excellence from the Associated Press. He lives with his wife and three children.